Wood Fired Ceramic Pots

By

Felicity McCullough

Series: Learn Something New

Black and White Illustrated

Wood Fired Ceramic Pots

Copyright

Copyright 2015 My Lap Shop Publishers

All Rights Reserved

No part of this publication may be reproduced, stored in a retrieval system, or transmitted in any form or by any means, electronic, mechanical, photocopying, recording, scanning, or otherwise, without the prior written permission of the Publisher. Requests to the Publisher for permission should be addressed to:

My Lap Shop Publishers

91 Mayflower Street, Unit 222, Plymouth, Devon PL1 1SB, United Kingdom

Wood Fired Ceramic Pots

Published by:

My Lap Shop Publishers

91 Mayflower Street, Unit 222,
Plymouth, Devon PL1 1SB,
United Kingdom
Tel: +44 (0)871 560 5297
www.mylapshop.com

About My Lap Shop Publishers

First Edition July 2015

Black & White Illustrated Paperback

ISBN: 978-1-78165-077-6

Wood Fired Ceramic Pots

Table of Illustrations

1 Art Portrait of Svend Bayer by Felicity McCullough   11
2 Art Illustration of Cathedral Style Wood Fired Kiln by Felicity McCullough   19
3 Art Illustration Wood Fired Glazed Jug by Felicity McCullough   21
4 Art Illustration of Scallop Shell by Felicity McCullough   24
5 Art Illustration of Bellamine Jar by Felicity McCullough   26
6 Photograph of a Wood Log Pile by Felicity McCullough   28
7 Art Illustration Stoking the Kiln by Felicity McCullough   31
8 Art Illustration Pile of Stoneware Clay by Felicity McCullough   42
9 Art Illustration Throwing a Pot by Felicity McCullough   42
10 Art Illustration Wood Fired Pot by Felicity McCullough   50
11 Art Illustration Chawan by Felicity McCullough   55
12 Cartoon of Svend Bayer by Felicity McCullough   58

Wood Fired Ceramic Pots

Wood Fired Ceramic Pots

Contents

Wood Fired Ceramic Pots	1
Series: Learn Something New	1
Black and White Illustrated	1
Copyright	2
Published by:	3
About My Lap Shop Publishers	3
Table of Illustrations	4
Contents	6
Introduction	8
The First Decade Project	10
Svend Bayer	11
Brannam Pottery	13
Far East	15
Wood Fired Kilns	15
Kiln Construction	19
Ash	23
Shells	24
Wood	27
Stoking the Kiln	29
Kiln Temperature	32
Wood Fired Pots	35
Exhibiting Pots	37
Business Strategy	38
Clay	41
Throwing Pots	42
Glazing	44
Colours	50
Decoration	54

Conclusion 56
Index 59
About Felicity McCullough 61
Other Publications 62
Published by: 63
About My Lap Shop Publishers
63

Wood Fired Ceramic Pots

Introduction

This book is based around the work of Svend Bayer a potter who has developed his skills through a passion in creating ceramic pots in a wood fired kiln.

Felicity McCullough has compiled and gathered the information from a variety of sources and from listening to Svend Bayer speak and talk about his life and work.

The pots created are individual and unique, as each pot is hand-crafted and the firing process creates the individualistic final piece of work, during the firing process.

Wood Fired Ceramic Pots

It is hoped that you will learn something new and enjoy reading about the work of Svend Bayer.

The colour illustrations and portrait are based on Felicity's artistic interpretations from a variety of visual sources.

There are also many images available to you on the web of his work and the hand-crafted pots.

Wood Fired Ceramic Pots

The First Decade Project

The Craft Council is working on developing a history of ceramics and creating an online archive, starting with the period 1972 to 1982, in the South and West.

Notable potters who have built reputations in the past and present day have included William Cookworthy, Bernard Leach, Svend Bayer and Malcolm Cardew.

The Craft Council setting up was supported by Lord Eccles, retired Paymaster General.

Wood Fired Ceramic Pots

Svend Bayer

Svend Bayer, potter, received a bursary from the Crafts Council in 1982, which helped set him on his path to spending his life throwing and creating pots, both large and small.

1 Art Portrait of Svend Bayer by Felicity McCullough

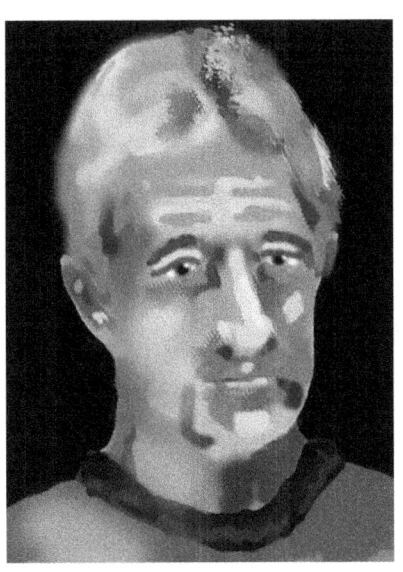

Wood Fired Ceramic Pots

After gaining his geography degree in 1968, Svend wanted to work with Malcolm Cardew at Wenford Bridge Pottery. He financed this through going to work in Denmark and during this period undertook a variety of jobs.

The three and a half years spent as an apprenticeship with Malcom Cardew, were challenging. It was an unpaid role. Also Malcolm's personality and characteristics were quite demanding.

Svend learnt the skills needed to fire large pots in wood fired kilns. Through receiving much encouragement from Michael

Cardew, Svend regarded his mentor as a perfect teacher.

By observation and practice, Svend taught himself to master the craft. This period laid the foundations for what he has achieved since.

Brannam Pottery

After gaining a good grounding in making pots, Svend moved to Barnstaple in North Devon to work for Clive Bowen, at Brannam Pottery.

Here, he learnt much from two fellow potters Bill and Frank, which further fuelled his passion for the craft. Bill's expertise lay in making small pots, and Frank specialised in making large pots. Frank took an interest in Svend and pushed him to excel. Svend further developed his pottery skills and knowledge under their guidance.

The pottery methods used are based on the history and past traditions of pottery, to which Svend has developed and crafted his own personal style.

Svend, who was from a Danish heritage, spoke little, as it was assumed he wasn't able to speak English. At Brannam Pottery, the community was divided, which was comprised of locals and Londoners that resulted in friction and opposing points of view.

Wood Fired Ceramic Pots

Far East

Having saved some money again Svend, embarked on another adventure to travel through Trans-Siberia to Japan, going through Korea and South-East Asia, learning all he could about ceramics.

These travels gave him insights into differences between the cultures and the history of throwing pots in many countries, as well as an understanding of how food and pottery are intricately linked.

Wood Fired Kilns

Based on the Japanese Anagama style of kiln firings,

Wood Fired Ceramic Pots

Svend has constructed many of his own enormous cave-like wood fired kilns.

Having his own large kilns, has helped and allowed him to choose his forte and undertake work on a large scale. Working mostly alone, the size of pots are limited to what he is able to lift.

On returning from his East Asia travels, in 1974 travelled to Connecticut in the United States.

Despite extreme cold weather, using bricks, he learnt how to construct a large-sized kiln, comprised of 10,000 bricks. It was 34 foot by 6 foot and 5 foot high in dimensions.

Wood Fired Ceramic Pots

The locale provided a good source of wood, which was to be used to fire the kiln. He was there from April to August and fired up the kiln twice. After his working permit expired, he returned to the UK, with his girlfriend.

Soon after, Svend looked for a suitable property where he could set up a kiln and run his own business. It was essential to have near-by access to wood and quality clay.

He found such a property at Duckpool, near Beaworthy in Devon.

Quickly he gained the necessary planning permission and with the bursary from the Craft Council, set about building his 240 cubic foot kiln.

In the first year he was profitable and never looked back thereafter.

Both of Svend's sons were born there.

Svend was able to focus on and specialised in creating large pots and has gained an international reputation through doing so.

Svend Bayer has operated as a self-sufficient potter, building his own kilns, creating and making his own glazes, as well as growing and using his own timber for the firings.

Kiln Construction

Over the years Svend has built many wood fired kilns.

2 Art Illustration of Cathedral Style Wood Fired Kiln by Felicity McCullough

The firing of pots in the wood kilns takes between 5 to 6 days. Svend Bayer currently uses two cross-draught wood fired kilns, which are housed in open-ended sheds.

The kilns are conveniently located adjacent to where the wood is stacked, making stoking easy.

The kilns are arranged in sections, with the large pots placed at the front of the kilns by the fire-boxes, which is the best place and the choicest place in the kiln, whilst at the same time being the most high risk place due to fire-flares. Big pots are the most difficult to fire successfully.

The sides of the kiln walls have stoke-holes. This facilitates maintaining a more even temperature throughout the kiln. It is where the larger jugs and round jars are placed.

3 Art Illustration Wood Fired Glazed Jug by Felicity McCullough

The smaller pots, jugs and bowls are arranged and placed towards the rear of the kiln.

Wood Fired Ceramic Pots

For four out of five days of firing wood is stoked onto and around the pots. Many do not survive. Pots are continuously buried in embers, emerging only to be buried once again in the firing cycle.

Arranging of pots within the kiln is important for several reasons.

During the stoking, the embers accumulate burying the pots until turning to ash, which eventually melts and flows over and between the pots. This can weld pots together if they are not adequately spaced. Once welded they are totally useless.

Svend wood fired kilns are built like a mini-cathedral of domed brick construction, from which takes much effort to get right. The design and construction has been based on his years of experience of what works best for wood fired kilns.

Ash

Over the 5 to 6 days much ash is created, which melts and flows as a liquid. This creates glazes, colours and patterns over the surface of the pots.

Embers turn into ash. Ash in turn melts and runs down the pot surface turning into a glass, and gives the fired pot when stood erect, a sense of movement horizontally and shine. Consequently, the surface of the pots become adorned with rivulets and drips.

If the pots were placed on a surface they would also become welded to that surface. Spacing between pots is important, otherwise pots become welded to each other, by solidification after liquids have flowed between pots within the kiln.

Shells

4 Art Illustration of Scallop Shell by Felicity McCullough

Wood Fired Ceramic Pots

In the kiln the pots are supported by sea-shells, which also in turn impregnate curvy patterns onto the pots surfaces, akin to the shape of the shell as fossils.

Shells are used, as they are able to withstand the high temperatures. When removed from the kiln the shells are broken off from the pot.

Three or four shells support the pots on the supporting parametric cones, with in the kiln. Shells can also be used to prevent adjacent pots from sticking together. The use of shells is practical and leaves a decorative fossil record of itself, on the pot's surface.

Wood Fired Ceramic Pots

Bellamine jars are sited in the kiln by being fired on its back, in a side-stoke area of the kiln. The side-stoke holes deposit ash onto the front of the pots from above, making the front of the jar decorative and appealing.

5 Art Illustration of Bellamine Jar by Felicity McCullough

Also, when pots explode in the kiln, they send shards over the remaining pots, impacting surfaces, potentially ruining everything that is being fired.

Wood

Svend maintains his wood-stack with much preciseness, to ensure that he has ample wood and in convenience places, for the firings. He chops, cuts and sorts and stacks with precision, well before starting any fire in the kiln.

Therefore, preparation is essential before firing the kiln, as the wood needs to be totally dry, for the marathon of the stoking.

Wood Fired Ceramic Pots

6 Photograph of a Wood Log Pile by Felicity McCullough

Initially Svend sourced the wood he used locally, however over time it has become more difficult to source, as local timber cutting businesses ceased to trade.

Consequently, he has needed to plant and grow his own trees.

In the past he has used Douglas Fir trees for the stoking, however when his source dried-up he had to find a new source.

Of late Svend now uses Poplars.

A 6-day firing takes 26 big poplar trees. So there is a lot of wood to source, cut and chop and stack in preparation, before he can start firing up the kiln, in order to create the pots needed to support his livelihood.

Stoking the Kiln

Svend works mainly alone. He achieves the firing with the support and help of apprentices, friends and family, which are needed for the firings, to keep the cross-draft kiln stoked over so many days.

He has two people to help during the firings, as it is over such a long period. Also round the clock stoking and attention to the kiln is needed. It is undertaken in shifts, of 4 hours on, with eight hours off.

This is challenging and needs much focus and care, giving the kiln constant attention to ensure the ash, embers and stoking maintain the heat throughout the kiln. Many pots do not survive the firing.

Wood Fired Ceramic Pots

7 Art Illustration Stoking the Kiln by Felicity McCullough

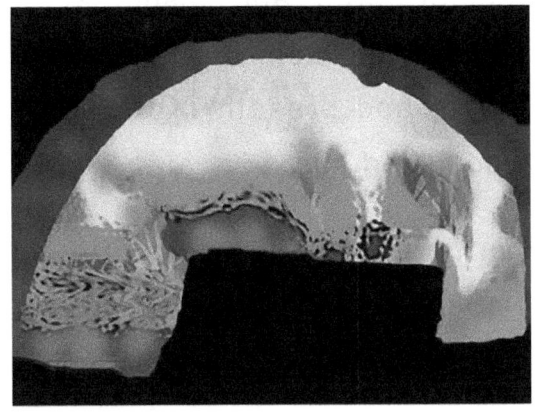

Also care is needed to ensure pots are not pushed over during the stoking by the insertion of the logs of wood.

Part of the stoker's role is to stir up embers for hours on end, to ensure as much ash is released onto the surfaces of the pots.

Giving attention to side-stoking is important, to ensure all areas of the kiln benefit from the high temperatures and dispersal of embers and ash, throughout the length and breadth of the large wood fired kiln.

For four out of five days of firing wood is stoked onto and around the pots.

If the stoking goes awry and oxidisation occurs, the resulting colours can be very dull. As the kiln is packed with hundreds of pots, there is much effort and profit at risk.

Kiln Temperature

Svend has experimented with getting the temperature of the kiln right. It is very challenging to get temperature evenly spread throughout the kiln.

The pots are placed in the kiln first and the fire is built up gradually to reach the ideal temperature.

Pots can easily explode and break, if the momentum of the firing isn't regulated correctly and evenly.

Ideally the kiln needs a temperature of 500 degrees centigrade. However, at 573 degrees centigrade silica expand and pots break, making side stoke-holes preferable, so that stoking may take place from the top.

Wood Fired Ceramic Pots

When the Silica expands a flame hits the pot, expansion and contraction takes place and results in a crack right down the front of the pot.

When stoking ceases the kiln cools down, which also requires regulation of temperature to avoid pots breaking. If the temperature varies significantly quickly, this can cause the pots to crack, frustratingly ruining the firing towards the end of the process.

On occasions, Svend has lost 80% of the pots through breakages, in one firing.

At these high temperatures ash itself will melt and form a glass glaze over the surface of the pot.

Wood Fired Pots

Throughout the firing, ash and embers are constantly being deposited onto the surface of the pots. This changes the appearance, colours and glazes on the surface. If boiling occurs then this also leaves its own unique blemishes.

Embers build up immersing the pots totally, until the ash melts and forms rivulets onto the surface and flows in the direction of gravity over the pots surface, which may be laid on its side, or in the case of a jug its front. Over the five to six days, this means that the pots become covered and then directly re-exposed to more embers and ash, repeating the cycle.

Svend is skilled at placing pots within the kiln where the glazing will be most effective, as he understands from experience where better results will be achieved.

Embers also leave their imprint on the pots. Oxidation also occurs, which gives differing effects around the external surfaces of the pots, resulting in a bright side and a dark side, as well as intertwined with the flow marks of the melted ash.

Wood Fired Ceramic Pots

Depending on which surface is on top, which is on the bottom and which area is placed facing into the centre of the kiln, impacts the final creation, and how the pot ultimately looks.

The craft is traditional and a dying art, one which has been around for over a thousand years.

Exhibiting Pots

Svend has exhibited widely in Europe, the Middle East, North America and Australia, and is one of the few remaining large pot potters, in the world.

Svend hopes that people find life and brightness in his pots, which are also glazed on the inside. He aims to provoke the desire in people to touch and hold his creations. His reputation, skill and craftsmanship is admired widely.

Svend has developed his techniques based on his many years of potting, however likes to ensure that his individuality is encompassed and shows through into his creations.

Business Strategy

Svend Bayer's business strategy was based on building a 600 cubic square foot kiln, so that he could make lots of pots and sell them at a price people would buy them at. He wanted buyers to be able to make practical use of the pots on a day-to-day basis.

Few others specialise in creating big pots giving Svend competitive advantage. Larger pots command higher prices and can be expensive. This is fully justified due to the amount of effort and materials needed to create them.

Storage of large pots are also challenging, as they need space and are always at risk of being broken before being sold.

Firing wood is very time consuming and expensive.

Svend has promoted, marketed and sold his pots directly,

through shops and galleries. He attends craft fairs, giving demonstrations of how he throws a pot.

Svend has exhibited in exhibitions. He has spoken about his life and how he has developed his international reputation, as a large-pot potter using the use of traditional methods of wood fired kilns, both in person and through media.

From home, Svend holds a sale and annual viewing of his work, making locals and those who come from further afield welcome.

Wood Fired Ceramic Pots

Clay

Obtaining local stoneware clay has been important to Svend. He has benefited by the proximity to the ball-clay mines at Peters Marland and Meeth in North Devon.

Svend also has his sandy clay made for him, in St. Agnes in Cornwall.

Svend includes at least one experimental clay in each of his firings and usually fires the pot, after dipping in a Kaki glaze.

Wood Fired Ceramic Pots

8 Art Illustration Pile of Stoneware Clay by Felicity McCullough

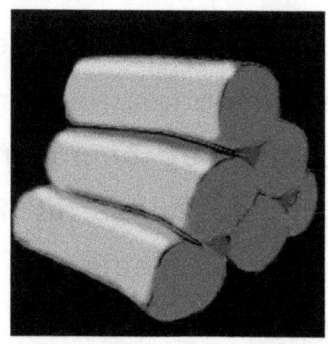

Throwing Pots

9 Art Illustration Throwing a Pot by Felicity McCullough

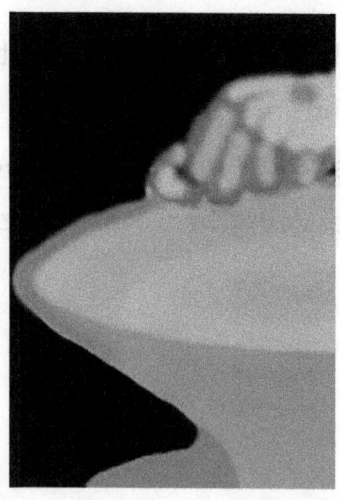

Wood Fired Ceramic Pots

Svend is skilled and experienced in throwing pots. Much strength is needed to throw big pots.

The large pots are built up with layers of coils of clay, added at each stage of the throwing. This can involve three to four coils of clay being added. It increases the weight of pots and can make these large items more susceptible to breakages, before during and after firing. The size is limited to what can be practically lifted.

The neck of the large pot or jar, can be challenging, because if it is not thrown quite right the whole object looks wrong, and can make the creation look out of balance.

The layers between the coils and surface are sealed by applying heat from a blow torch.

Glazing

Glazing is time consuming and expensive to do. Glazing has become important to Svend, which enhances the look and feel of his pots.

The material used and glazes are slightly caustic and harsh on the hands.

Celadon glazes are applied to provide a transparent glaze of the pot. The glaze is produced in a wide variety of colours and may be applied to the internal and external surfaces in varying thicknesses. It also combines with the clay used to influence the resulting final shade of the pot.

The glazes are fired in a reducing atmosphere kiln, such as a wood fired kiln, which allows chemical changes to occur to the iron oxide, as the Celadon glaze is deprived of oxygen during the intense heat firing, to produce colours needed. Carbon trapping of the Celadon colours occur.

A Celadon liner glaze changes to a wonderful blue colour, when exposed to ash.

Crazing can occur to the glaze whilst in the firing process and can result in a crackle effect on the surface of the pots.

Svend uses Celadon glazes made from local rocks, which include granite.

Also used are popular Shino glazes, which have their origins in Japan. The Shino glazes primarily use feldspar and a small amount of clay with many different colorants and fluxes added.

Spotting of the surface can also be achieved with Shino glazes, which is known as beading.

Shino glazes reacts particularly well with wood ash. Svend also achieves great results in the wood fired kiln, as amazing transformation in the Shino glaze takes place using his wood and ash methods.

Kaki glazes are high fired reduction transparent, with a 12% or more iron oxide content. The Kaki glaze forms a microcrystalline surface over the pot. When cooled correctly, they result in reddish colouration.

Through use and experimentation with Celadon, Shino and Kaki glazes and through exposing these glazes to the wood ash in the wood fired kiln, Svend achieves some new and dazzling results.

Wood Fired Ceramic Pots

Kaki undergoes the most profound changes, when exposed to ash. When the ash lands and combines with it, initially it first turns black and shiny. As ash accumulates over the length of the wood firing, colours of blue, yellow, green and silver streaks form.

The ash itself also melts and makes a glaze. Ash changes the composition of the applied glazes by reacting, resulting in a variety of pleasing visual effects.

All these glazes are traditionally protected from kiln ash, however Svend achieves startling colours and creates the feel of movement on the pots surfaces, through exposing the glazes directly to the ash.

Under the wood fired kiln temperature reduction process, glazes can boil. The bubbles created during boiling leaves the evidence that boiling has occurred on the surface in the form of a broken surface, akin to the surface of the moon. These blisters may also scar the final appearance of the pot.

The results of the glaze having boiled, are suitable for the exterior of pots. However boiling indentations would be unsuitable and unacceptable for interior surfaces of pots, which are intended for food and used in eating.

Wood Fired Ceramic Pots

Prolonged exposure to high temperatures, embers and ash completely changes the Celadon, Shino and Kaki glazes, giving extraordinary colours and movement in the pots final presentation and appearance.

Colours

10 Art Illustration Wood Fired Pot by Felicity McCullough

Wood Fired Ceramic Pots

Resulting glaze colours can vary in range and shade. This can melt in tints of blue, green and grey on the pot's surface. It occurs randomly during the firing process.

The resulting colours depend on the type of wood used, the embers and ash, the chemical properties of the glaze, all of which have come into contact with the pot in the firing processes.

The colour results are also significantly influenced by the siting and orientation of the pot within the kiln, during the firing.

In the kiln, the pots become buried and then re-exposed, as

the ash becomes liquid, in a continual cycle of change. Sitting for long periods in the embers, creates darker coloured areas on the surfaces of the pots being fired.

The colours also mix with the colours of the clay used to throw the pot. The red body of the pot melds with the embers and ash, especially when in liquid form to provide an overall cool glaze.

This also gives the pot a differing look from the side exposed to the heat and falling ash, from the side below, which sits in the embers, making each pot unique. When looked at from a different perspective it looks like a completely different pot.

Wood Fired Ceramic Pots

When ash combines with Celadon glaze, other resulting colours ensue such as an optical blue, yellow, off-white and green.

By stirring up embers at the front of the kiln the front receives all of the ash. Those pots at the front will have brightness of colour and be attractive to touch, creating a desire to hold and feel the pot surface, making the pot very tactile and attractive.

The pots towards the back of the kiln result in pot colours, which are far more muted.

As pots are buried in embers for three of the four-day firings, frequent changes of colours and textures occur.

Decoration

Decorative marks may be applied to the surfaces of the pots.

Svend Bayer uses his own Potters Mark.

Svend paints a decoration on the exterior surface of his Japanese style tea bowls, a type of Chawan, using iron pigment, before dipping the Chawan in a glaze and firing.

Wood Fired Ceramic Pots

11 Art Illustration Chawan by Felicity McCullough

Because of the wood fired method used, pots have scars and blemishes, which come directly from the firing process itself.

Conclusion

Wood fired pots are therefore uniquely individual, even from different perspectives of the same pot.

Outcomes from wood fired kilns are unpredictable, making each firing a real gamble.

Some pots get knocked over. Some creations become broken. Others end up sticking together and end up being smashed and discarded. Occasionally a pot will explode, showering shards over its neighbours. If a pot survives all of the above, it still may not produce a desired appearance and appeal, and potentially have to be re-glazed

Wood Fired Ceramic Pots

and re-fired. With losses this dauntingly high, it is a marvel that any make it through the wood firing process, to end up for sale. When they do, they are an object of absolute beauty and delight.

By looking at a pot, much is revealed of what happened during its throwing, glazing and firing. Each bit of the pot tells an interesting story of its history, in its own right.

Svend Bayer has demonstrated a real passion for creating ceramics that are ethical, pleasing and are sought after.

Through my research I have also discovered that Svend Bayer

gained a strong reputation as a cartoonist, whilst at school. Therefore, I couldn't resist producing my own version of a cartoon of him, created from my colour portrait of him.

12 Cartoon of Svend Bayer by Felicity McCullough

Index

Anagama 15
Bayer, Svend 8, 9, 10, 11, 18, 19, 38, 54, 57, 58
Bellamine Jars 26
Boiling..................................35, 49
Brannam Pottery 13, 14
Cardew, Malcolm....................10, 12
Cartoon 58
Celadon...........44, 45, 46, 47, 50, 53
Chawan 54, 55
Clay 17, 41, 43, 45, 46, 52
Colours 23, 32, 35, 44, 45, 48, 50, 51, 52, 53, 54
Cookworthy, William 10
Craft Council....................... 10, 18
Crazing 45
Decoration 54
Douglas Fir................................. 29
Firings....... 15, 19, 27, 29, 30, 41, 53
Glaze . 35, 41, 44, 45, 47, 48, 49, 51, 52, 53, 54
Glazing................................36, 57
Kaki 41, 47, 48, 50
Kiln .8, 15, 16, 17, 18, 20, 21, 22, 24, 25, 26, 27, 29, 30, 32, 33, 34, 36, 37, 38, 45, 47, 48, 49, 51, 53
Kiln Construction......................... 19
Leach, Bernard 10
McCullough................................. 61
My Lap Shop Publishers 2, 3, 62, 63

Wood Fired Ceramic Pots

Oxidation 36
Plymouth 2, 3, 63
Poplars 29
Potters Mark 54
Shells 24, 25
Shino 46, 47, 50
Silica 33
Stoking 20, 22, 27, 29, 30, 31, 32, 33, 34
Temperature 21, 32, 33, 34, 49
Throwing 11, 15, 43, 57
Wenford Bridge Pottery 12
Wood Fired. 8, 12, 16, 19, 22, 23, 32, 40, 45, 47, 49, 55, 56
Wood Fired Kilns .. 12, 16, 19, 22, 23, 40, 56

About Felicity McCullough

Felicity McCullough has a wide variety of interests and has been taking photographs for many years, as well as illustrating and painting. A keen photographer, Felicity has published some of her photographs in bite-sized glimpses in her series *'Places to Visit'*.

'Wood Fired Ceramic Pots' is the first in her series *'Learn Something New'*.

Whilst researching and writing the book, Felicity has gained a great deal of knowledge and in this short and easy to read publication, she shares this important material with you, as wood firing of large pots, is becoming a dying craft.

Felicity has illustrated the subject matter herself, in her own artistic style, which adds further interest to the subject matter.

The book is available both as a colour illustrated paperback, and as a black and white illustrated paperback. It is also available as an e-Book, all of which are available through Amazon's website.

Books in the series: *Places to Visit*: -

> Chester A Photographic Glimpse
>
> Newton Abbot A Photographic Glimpse

Other Publications

Additionally, Felicity McCullough has written several books about '*Preventative Health Care*' for goats. The website www.goatlapshop.com has a wide variety of topics and resources that relate to goats, including other guides in the '*Goat Knowledge Series*'.

The '*Charlie And Isabella's Magical Adventures*' Series of Children's Books, about the adventures of two magical goats, which are suitable for bedtime reading and are beautifully illustrated, are also available from the Publisher My Lap Shop Publishers.

Wood Fired Ceramic Pots

Published by:

My Lap Shop Publishers

91 Mayflower Street, Unit 222,
Plymouth, Devon PL1 1SB,
United Kingdom
Tel: +44 (0)871 560 5297

www.mylapshop.com

About My Lap Shop Publishers

Black and White Edition July 2015

www.ingramcontent.com/pod-product-compliance
Lightning Source LLC
Chambersburg PA
CBHW071501160426
43195CB00013B/2173